EARTH DAY — HOORAY!

by Stuart J. Murphy • illustrated by Renée Andriani

HarperCollins Publishers

LEVEL 3

To Mark McVeigh—
a big hooray for suggesting Earth Day
—S.J.M.

For Stuart, of course
—R.A.

The publisher and author would like to thank teachers Patricia Chase, Phyllis Goldman, and
Patrick Hopfensperger for their help in making the math in MathStart just right for kids.

HarperCollins®, ♟ ®, and MathStart® are registered trademarks of HarperCollins Publishers.
For more information about the MathStart series,
For information address HarperCollins Children's Books, a division of HarperCollins Publishers,
10 East 53rd Street, New York, NY 10022,
or visit our website at www.mathstartbooks.com.

Bugs incorporated in the MathStart series design were painted by Jon Buller.

Library of Congress Cataloging-in-Publication Data
Murphy, Stuart J.
    Earth Day—hooray! / by Stuart J. Murphy ; illustrated by Renée
Andriani. — 1st ed.
        p. cm. — (MathStart)
"Place value."
"Level 3."
Summary: A drive to recycle cans on Earth Day teaches the children of the Maple Street School
Save-the-Planet Club about place value.
    ISBN 0-06-000127-5 — ISBN 0-06-000129-1 (pbk.)
    1. Place value (Mathematics)—Juvenile literature. 2. Recycling (Waste, etc.)—Juvenile
literature. [1. Place value (Mathematics) 2. Recycling (Waste, etc.)] I. Andriani, Renée, ill.
II. Title. III. Series.
    QA141.M87 2004
    513—dc21
                                                                                          2002155234

Typography by Elynn Cohen   11 12 13 SCP 10   ❖ First Edition

"This place is a mess," said Ryan.

"That's why we're cleaning it up," said Carly. "C'mon, pitch in!"

The Maple Street School Save-the-Planet Club was cleaning up Gilroy Park, the site of this year's Earth Day celebration. They picked up candy wrappers, crumpled newspaper, empty coffee cups, old flyers, lost tennis balls, and lots of aluminum cans.

In 1999, recycling and composting kept about 64,000,000,000 (64 billion) tons of trash from ending up in landfills or being burned (which pollutes the air).

"You know," said Ryan, "even after we're finished cleaning the park, it won't look all that great. It could really use some flowers at the entrance." Gilroy Park had a few trees and some grass—and that was it.

6

"If we take all these cans to the recycling center instead of throwing them away," Ryan continued, "they'll give us money for each can. Maybe we can make enough to buy some flowers to plant!"

Mrs. Watson, the club adviser, thought Ryan's idea was fantastic. She said, "If you can get 5,000 cans, that should be enough for some really beautiful flowers."

"I bet we won't find that many," said Luke.

Companies pay recyclers about $1,000,000,000 (1 billion) a year to buy aluminum.

The club sorted all the cans they found. Ryan, Carly, and Luke filled small bags with 10 cans each. When they had 10 small bags, they put them in a big bag that held 100 cans so they would be easier to count.

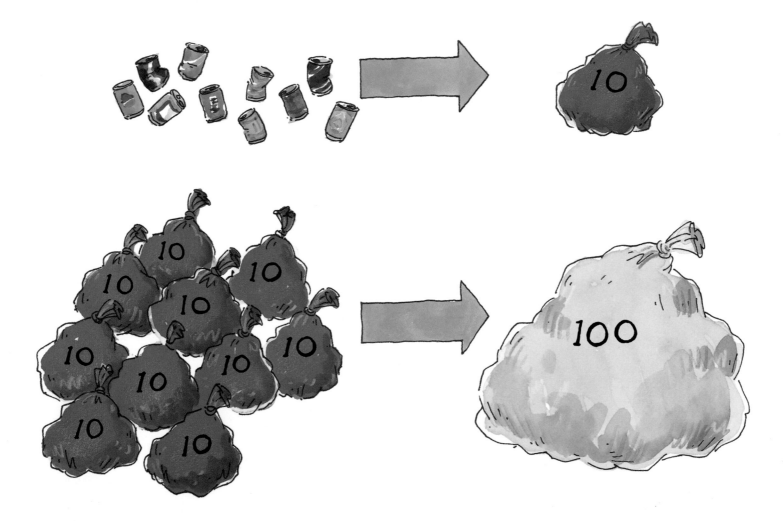

They ended up with three big bags of 100, five small bags of 10, and nine single cans.

They left the bags near the trash bins so that Mrs. Watson could pick them up that evening.

But the next morning at school, Mrs. Watson called Ryan, Carly, and Luke to her desk.

"Bad news," she said. "The trash collector at the park didn't realize the cans were for recycling. He took them to the dump with the rest of the trash."

"I knew it," said Luke. "I knew we'd never do it!"

"Don't give up!" said Ryan. "We can still collect cans. We'll have a can drive right here at school!"

"I don't know," said Luke doubtfully. "It will only work if a lot of people bring in cans."

Americans use more than 80,000,000,000 (80 billion) aluminum cans a year.

Americans save 247,000,000 (247 million) pounds of paper every day to be reused and recycled.

14

The custodian, Mrs. Jones, set up a barrel in the hallway. Luke made a big sign.

Mrs. Watson helped Ryan print up a flyer announcing their goal. Carly drew a cartoon.

15

The next day a few kids brought in cans. After school Ryan, Carly, and Luke went to check out the barrel.
They sorted the cans into bags. They had five small bags of 10, and six single cans.

Carly wrote "56" on the sign. "We need to get more kids to help," she said.

Carly, Luke, and Ryan got permission to visit every class and ask for help with the can drive. Carly worked all night so she would be ready.

In the year 2000, Americans recycled 1,900,000,000 (1 billion, 900 million) pounds of aluminum.

WE CAN DO IT!

The first Earth Day celebration was on April 22, 1970. About 20,000,000 (20 million) people participated.

After school, Ryan, Carly, and Luke stopped at every park and field and picked up every can they saw.

The next morning Ryan, Carly, and Luke brought their cans to school. They went by the barrel to drop them off.

"Look at all these cans!" said Carly. "I knew it would work!"

At recess they counted the cans. They ended up with six big bags of 100, three small bags of 10, and five single cans.

Carly wrote the total on the sign.

Mrs. Watson walked by. "You're going to need bigger bags," she said. "I'll bring some in tomorrow."

And we had 56 yesterday, so added up it's 691!

When Ryan, Carly, and Luke checked the barrel the next day, it was overflowing. "We'd better ask Mrs. Jones for some more barrels," said Carly.

They had one bag of 1,000, four bags of 100, eight bags of 10, and three single cans.

That's 1,483!

1,000

100

100

100

Carly wrote the total on the sign and remembered to put
a comma between the thousands and the hundreds.

Ryan, Carly, and Luke kept working. Luke put signs up all over school. On Saturday the members of the Save-the-Planet Club knocked on every door in their neighborhoods. They handed out Ryan's flyer and carried big bags for people's empty cans.

Recycling 1 aluminum can saves enough energy to keep a 100-watt lightbulb burning for about 3½ hours.

On Monday morning, Ryan, Carly, and Luke couldn't dump their cans in the collection barrels—because they were already full.

At recess they counted cans. By the time recess was over they still weren't done. Mrs. Watson said they could skip spelling to finish counting.

"And you didn't think this was a good idea," Carly teased Luke.

Finally they finished. They had two huge bags of 1,000, eight big bags of 100, five small bags of 10, and two single cans.

Luke wrote the numbers down. "We did it!" he shouted.

And with the 2,174 we had before... it's 5,026!

EARTH DAY - HOORAY!
Cans recycled so far:
5,026
HELP US REACH OUR GOAL OF 5,000
nt flowers in Gilroy Park!

Mrs. Watson took the cans to the recycling center right after school. And Saturday morning she drove Carly, Luke, and Ryan to the plant nursery. They each picked out flowers in their favorite colors.

CARE For the AIR

Plant a TREE!

Earth Day - Hooray!

Water Ecosystem

That afternoon the whole class came to Gilroy Park for the Earth Day celebration. The first thing they did was plant the flowers at the entrance.

The park looked beautiful. And there wasn't a single piece of trash anywhere.

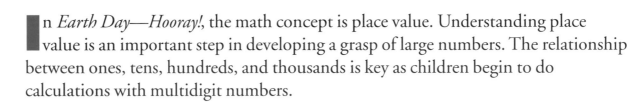
In *Earth Day—Hooray!*, the math concept is place value. Understanding place value is an important step in developing a grasp of large numbers. The relationship between ones, tens, hundreds, and thousands is key as children begin to do calculations with multidigit numbers.

If you would like to have more fun with the math concepts presented in *Earth Day—Hooray!*, here are a few suggestions:

- As you read the story with the child, point out how the cans are bundled together in groups of 10s, 100s, and 1000s. Discuss with the child how 10 ones equal 10, 10 tens equal 100, and 10 hundreds equal 1,000.

- Retell the story, making up different amounts of cans collected. For example, tell the child that the characters have collected 5 bags of 100, 6 bags of 10, and 3 single cans. Have the child write the number and keep track of how many cans were collected.

- Write down a 3-digit number and have the child draw bundles of cans to represent the number.

- Write the digits from 0 to 9 on ten paper plates. Turn the plates over, have the child choose 4 of them, and then turn them face up. Ask questions like, "What is the biggest number you could make?" "What is the smallest number?" Discuss the place value of the numbers created. (For example, if the child makes the number 1,259, point out that this number has 1 thousand, 2 hundreds, 5 tens, and 9 ones.)

Following are some activities that will help you extend the concepts presented in *Earth Day—Hooray!* into a child's everyday life:

Recycling: Discuss with the child items that he or she can recycle, like newspapers or cans. Set a goal for the number of items to recycle, perhaps 100 cans or 100 newspapers. Have the child keep track of the number collected and how many items he or she still needs to meet the goal.

Guess the Number: Think of a 3-digit number (all 3 digits should be different). Have the child guess the number, and then tell him or her which digits are correct but in the wrong place and which digits are correct and in the right place. (For example, if the number is 384 and the child guesses 412, you would say, "The 4 is correct, but it is in the wrong place.") Continue guessing until the number is found.

The following books include some of the same concepts that are presented in *Earth Day—Hooray!*:

- RECYCLE!: *A Handbook for Kids* by Gail Gibbons

- THE WARLORD'S BEADS by Virginia Walton Pilegard

- HOW MUCH IS A MILLION? by David M. Schwartz